AMERICA'S WORKHORSE

LOCOMOTIVE:

the 2-8-2

by

Robert A. LeMassena

© 1993 by Robert A. LeMassena
All rights reserved
Designed by Frederick A. Kramer
ISBN 0-915276-54-2

QUADRANT PRESS, INC.
19 West 44th Street
New York, NY 10036
[212-819-0822]

Rockton & Rion, Fairfield County, SC.   *John R. Krause*

ACKNOWLEDGEMENTS

There were more locomotives built to the 2-8-2 wheel arrangement than any other type having a trailing truck. Surprisingly, specific references to these locomotives are rare indeed. The best basic sources of specific information come, of course, from the builders' construction records and books relating to the major builders. While a number of publications do contain fragmentary general references to the 2-8-2, the detailed rosters published in railfan literature provide excellent information on specific 2-8-2s. *Railroad History, Railroad Magazine,* and *Trains* were valuable sources of information, as was George Hilton's *American Narrow Gauge Railroads* and the *Steam Passenger Service Directory.* Thanks goes to "Rocky" Haimowitz for sharing his copies of many of the magazine rosters.

To illustrate specific examples, most of the photographs come from Harold K. Vollrath whose outstanding collection contained virtually all of the portraits needed within narrow road-number and classification type ranges. His generous help in locating pictures that would best illustrate these engines is appreciated beyond measure.

Some of the photographs needed for completeness were unlisted in the Baldwin Locomotive Works negative collection. Benjamin F. G. Kline of the Pennsylvania State Railroad Museum diligently searched, found, and made these missing items available. Charles Albi of the Colorado Railroad Museum verified data in the museum's reference library, and Edward May, whose expertise on New York Central motive power is first class, provided a detailed compilation of that system's 2-8-2s.

The work of a number of other noted photographers showing 2-8-2s in action and selected photographs from collectors are included. Not all of the dates and locations were recorded from those long-ago days, but all of the available information is shown. Many of the names are familiar and not all are alive, but my sincere thanks go to each and every one: Donald Duke, H. F. Stewart, J. W. Maxwell, D. S. Richter, Gordon Roth, Dick George, C. W. Burns, Thomas T. Taber, John Krause, Ed Crist, Bob Penisi, August A. Thieme, Jr., Robert F. Collins, S. E. Herring, C. M. Clegg, William S. Young, Bruce Fales, and Richard H. Kindig.

Also, I cannot fail to acknowledge all of those whose advice and assistance behind the scenes has helped in the preparation of this account of the 2-8-2. Collectively, their contributions have formed what will, I hope, become a basic, though brief, reference on this specialized subject.

ROBERT A. LeMASSENA
Lakewood, CO., March, 1993

FRONT COVER:
One of the Erie's unheralded workhorses was No. 3203, one of fifteen 2-8-2s built by American during World War I. Its Worthington Type BL feedwater heater was added in the late 1920s when a program of upgrading the road's Mikados was undertaken. This view was taken October 14, 1950 at Wanaque-Midvale on the New York & Greenwood Lake line.   *Robert F. Collins*

INSIDE FRONT COVER:
Two of Louisville & Nashville's biggest 2-8-2s, seen lugging a heavy train of bituminous coal, were equipped with modern feedwater heaters and trailing truck boosters.   *Ed Crist collection*

TITLE PAGE:
Delaware, Lackawanna & Western's booster-equipped No. 2130 doubleheaded with 4-8-4 No. 1608 on a westbound merchandise train to climb the 1.7% grade at Mt. Pocono, PA. Another 2100 was pushing against the caboose at the rear of this unusually heavy consist.   *Robert A. LeMassena*

INSIDE BACK COVER:
No. 1409 typifies Missouri Pacific's standard heavy 2-8-2s in action, showing to good effect the huge boiler with its 91-inch diameter smokebox–largest of any 2-8-2.   *John R. Krause*

TABLE OF CONTENTS

FOREWORD

This book commenced as a casual inquiry into the identity of the first, heaviest, and last 2-8-2s constructed for service on North American railroads. The search quickly became frustrating because "reliable" sources of information were in obvious disagreement. Consequently, I decided to undertake a search of builders' and railroads' records to determine the truth of the matter. What I found was a series of surprises; and, I feel that anyone interested in steam locomotives will be equally surprised.

The first 2-8-2s were not those built by Baldwin in 1897 for the Nippon Railway. Sixteen 2-8-2s preceded them, with Baldwin itself having erected twelve of them between 1890 and 1893. The heaviest ones were not the ones which Baldwin delivered to the St. Louis-San Franciso in 1930, but 25 monsters which the Great Northern completed in its own shops between 1944 and 1946. The last North American 2-8-2s were produced in 1947 for the White Pass & Yukon (3' gauge), Canadian Pacific (standard gauge) in 1948, and the Newfoundland Railway (3-½' gauge) in 1949.

There was considerable variety among the 341 2-8-2s constructed between 1884 and 1909, when the first road-service locomotives were delivered to the Virginian. Twenty-eight railroads were involved, having nine different track gauges ranging from only 24 inches to 66 inches. Baldwin produced 134 locomotives, of which 46 were shipped to railroads in Peru, India, Mexico, Venezuela, Japan, Finland, and New Zealand. American and its predecessors erected 279, of which 180 went to the Northern Pacific and 47 to the Lehigh Valley. Eighteen engines were tank-types; 32 had Vauclain compound cylinders; 20 had crossover compound cylinders; and 47 had center cabs.

Not all of the 10,000 or so 2-8-2s which ran on North American railroads were constructed completely new. Many were modifications of some other wheel arrangement–2-6-2, 4-6-2, 2-8-0, 2-10-0, 2-10-2, and even 2-6+6-2, 2-6+8-0, and 2-8+8-2 articulateds. The 2-8-2 designed by the USRA in light and heavy versions was the most popular of eight standard wheel arrangements, and the quantity built was only four less than the total of all 682 of the others, except the two types of articulateds. American delivered 312 of the light 2-8-2; Baldwin was next with 183; and Lima's share of the total was 130. Two hundred and three of the heavy design came from American and 30

from Baldwin. It is interesting to note that the Pennsylvania Railroad's standard 2-8-2, 574 of which were erected between 1914 and 1917, was a reasonably close prototype. The smallest 2-8-2 weighed only 20 tons; the heaviest one, 213 tons; and driving wheels ranged from 28 to 70 inches.

The story of the development of the 2-8-2 commenced with the need for a rear truck to prevent derailments when a locomotive was operated backward. Next came the application of a large firebox (for burning wood or lignite) to a 2-8-0. The extra weight behind the rear axle required a trailing truck for adequate support. But it was not until 1909, when Baldwin built ten 2-8-2s for the Virginian, that a true road-service design appeared.

The Pennsylvania's design, first built in 1914, represented a significant advance–larger driver diameter and a larger grate area in a Belpaire firebox. The USRA models of 1919 resembled them, except for the radial-stay fireboxes. The maximum grate area–108 square feet–was attained on a non-articulated locomotive for the first time in 1912 when the Philadelphia & Reading's shops built a 2-8-2 which used slow-burning hard coal for locomotive fuel. In 1928, the Lehigh Valley converted several 2-10-2s with 100 sqft. grates to 2-8-2s, and the Great Northern's 2-8-2s rebuilt with new Belpaire firebox boilers during 1944-1946 came close to them at 98.5 sqft.

Although the 2-8-2 became the most useful road service steam locomotive, it was also a versatile industrial engine, capable of operating over the light track typical of mining and lumbering companies without having to turn the engine at the end of track. Although saddle-tanks were common equipment on smaller locomotives, a few 2-8-2s were built in this manner for lumber railroads in the 1920 decade. In this same period, several powerful narrow gauge locomotives were built for mainline freight and passenger service. Canadian and South American narrow gauge railroads used 2-8-2s for mainline trains, but Mexican railroads preferred 2-8-0s, and in several instances removed the trailing truck from new 2-8-2s.

Just as the last steam locomotives were being constructed for North American railroads in the early 1950s, many railroads had formulated plans for their complete replacement by diesel-electric units by the end of the decade. By 1965, the steam locomotive had vanished from the continent except for a few lumber companies and the narrow gauge lines of the Denver

& Rio Grande Western. The remarkable aspect of their operations was that all of the D&RGW's locomotives were 2-8-2s, as were several of those operated by the lumber companies! Equally remarkable was the existence of other narrow gauge 2-8-2s–in storage–on the East Broad Top, Newfoundland, Sumpter Valley, and White Pass & Yukon railroads. Except for these few 2-8-2s, North America was steamless for all practical purposes.

Then, in 1966, a modern miracle occurred. The Southern Railway bought back its first 2-8-2 which it had sold in 1948, the now famous 4501. Its operation in mainline excursion service marked the beginning of an entirely new aspect of modern railroading: the steam-powered excursion. Commencing with that early model 2-8-2, the steam revival now embraces powerful 2-8-4s, 4-8-4s, 2-6+6-2 lumber Mallets and the gigantic 2-6+6-4 and 4-6+6-4 single- expansion locomotives. And–believe it or not–Rio Grande, East Broad Top, and White Pass & Yukon narrow gauge 2-8-2s are still running!

Following the renaissance of Southern 4501, two other 2-8-2s–Burlington 4960 and Buffalo Creek & Gauley 17–were used in excursion service. Of these three pioneers, only the 4501 has survived.

Now, 25 years later, there are 130 2-8-2s which have escaped the scrapper's torch, and 39 of them are being operated by tourist railroads. Only twelve are standard gauge; 26 run on 3-foot gauge track; and one operates on 15-inch gauge.

Add to these totals three more standard gauge locomotives built just recently in China. In the list below the original owner and road number are shown. The engines do move around a bit, hence their present locations should be verified in a current issue of *Steam Passenger Service Directory.*

Aberdeen & Rockfish 40

Canadian National 3254

Coos Bay Lumber 11 – [Tank type]

Denver & Rio Grande 464 – [3' gauge]

Denver & Rio Grande Western 473, 476, 478, 480-484, 486-489,
492-495, 497-499 –[3' gauge]

East Broad Top 12, 14, 15, 17 – [3' gauge]

Grand Trunk Western 4070

Magma Arizona 7

McCloud River 19

New York, Chicago & St. Louis 587

Owen-Oregon Lumber 3

Paradise & Pacific 11 – [15'' gauge]

Port of Grays Harbor 5

Portland, Astoria & Pacific 102

Southern 4501

Southern Pacific (T&NO) 786

White Pass & Yukon 73, 190 – [3' gauge]

In addition, there are a couple of more 2-8-2s which are being restored for operation, but their completion dates are indefinite.

Bruce Fales

Southern Railway's newer 2-8-2s were near-duplicates of the USRA-heavy locomotives, and they hauled most of the mainline freight trains. This one was No. 4815 seen darkening the skies at Alexandria, Virginia in January of 1939.

IN THE BEGINNING: 1884-1909

THE NAME "MIKADO"

In that long ago era when stories about steam locomotives–particularly big and fast ones–appeared on the front pages of newspapers, the various wheel arrangements were generally known to the public by nicknames such as American, Atlantic, or Consolidation. These were type names for various wheel arrangements, used primarily by the press, the builders' sales departments, advertisers, and the public.

However, there were some locomotive wheel arrangements that had no type nicknames. Obviously, this was always the case when a new wheel arrangement was invented. When the first 2-8-2 appeared, Angus Sinclair, editor of *Railway & Locomotive Engineering,* attempted to name this new type the "Calumet." His proposed name derived from the fact that Brooks had built four engines of this configuration for the Chicago & Calumet Terminal railroad. Apparently lacking the sweep and scope of a type name such as Atlantic or missing an evolutionary implication of a type name such as Consolidation, his proposal was ignored and this first attempt at naming the 2-8-2 was unsuccessful.

Samuel Vauclain as general superintendent of the Baldwin Locomotive Works succeeded where Sinclair as an editor had failed. Vauclain christened the twenty 2-8-2s which his company built in 1897 for the Imperial Railway of Nippon as the "Mikado" type. Since Vauclain was also a partner in the Baldwin company, he saw to it that the sales department of the world's leading locomotive builder perpetuated the name. By the sheer force of Baldwin's weight in the business, the name stuck. The type would later became more popularly known as a "Mike."

During World War II, the public relations departments of a few railroads reacted to anti-Japanese sentiment. They tried to rename 2-8-2s as MacArthurs. Although this change was generally ignored, Union Pacific operating timetables showed the MacArthur designation until the end of the steam era in 1959, long after the old soldier had faded away.

Nevertheless, internal to the locomotive building industry, locomotives were identified by wheel arrangement, not type name. Bookkeepers also grouped locomotives by wheel arrangement, assigning a different class identification to each. Classes were designated by an alphabetic letter using suffix numerals and letters to designate mechanical variations. Thus, a railroad could have what it called a class D locomotive, or a D-16, or a D16sa, or whatever degree of differentiation was warranted in separating operating and maintenance expense to a particular group of motive power.

Railroads had other symbolic ways of identifying the 2-8-2s in their service. For example, Atchison, Topeka & Santa Fe spoke of a 4101 class engine, using the road number of the first in the class. The Chicago, Rock Island & Pacific referred to class K68B indicating both tractive effort and the presence of a booster. Denver & Rio Grande Western's class 125 was based on engine weight, and the numerals in Missouri Pacific's class MK63 referred to driver diameter. Great Northern used O8 to identify two mechanically different groups having identical road numbers!

Interestingly, regardless of how others in and out of the railroad industry referred to the motive power, those who operated and maintained the engines almost universally knew them by their individual road numbers.

THE BASIC DESIGN

Initially, the 2-8-2 locomotive was regarded as little more than a 2-8-0 which could be operated backwards reliably. But when the firebox was placed behind the driving wheels instead of above them, it became practicable to enlarge the firebox and increase the diameter of the drivers. The smaller models of 2-8-2s with the firebox above the drivers had wheel diameters in the range of 55 to 57 inches. The prevailing practice was to equip larger 2-8-2s with 63 inch drivers.

The 2-8-2's large firebox assured good steaming conditions, and grate areas were ample for efficient firing rates. Northern Pacific's early engines had 41 square feet, the limit for hand firing. The Pennsylvania's 71 square feet was the same as that of the USRA-heavy design, while New York Central's 67 square foot area matched the USRA's light 2-8-2. The more modern locomotives were provided with grate areas up to 106 square feet, but these largest ones used slow-burning anthracite. The USRA boilers had short combustion chambers which increased steam production, though there was a great variation–zero to two feet–on other designs.

The two modifications of a larger firebox and bigger drivers resulted in a remarkable improvement in performance. Compared to the 2-8-0, a 2-8-2 could be operated at higher speeds, produce more drawbar horsepower, and have greater lateral stability. Moreover, the 2-8-2 was easier on the track because the engine's weight was distributed over two equalized symmetrical axle groups (2-4=4-2).

These characteristics were ideal for freight service on the undulating profiles of the prairie railroads as well as for passenger service on railroads having severe gradients. A widespread practice was to equip a 2-8-2 with a trailing truck booster. This device gave a 2-8-2 the ability to start a heavier train that might otherwise require a 2-10-2. Moreover, once underway, a 2-8-2 could typically haul a train at higher speeds than a 2-10-2. Some railroads used trailing truck boosters extensively: New York Central, Chesapeake & Ohio, and Southern Pacific come quickly to mind. Other roads, such as the Pennsylvania, Southern, and Chicago, Burlington & Quincy, avoided them completely for various reasons which included first cost, maintenance requirements, and reliability.

THE ABSTAINERS

Despite the widespread acceptance and good performance of 2-8-2 locomotives everywhere, there were a number of large, and some major, railroads which did not acquire any 2-8-2s. In the Northeast, the Bangor & Aroostook, Boston & Maine, Central Vermont, Delaware & Hudson, Bessemer & Lake Erie, Long Island, and Quebec Central all failed to buy any. In the south and central regions, the same can be said for the Georgia & Florida, Richmond, Fredericksburg & Potomac, Norfolk & Western, Western Maryland, Toledo, Peoria & Western, St.

Recent Locomotives

In 1867, Norris constructed the first two 2-10-0s for the Lehigh Valley railroad which used them as pushers on freight trains. After enduring 13 years of excessive flange wear, the railroad rebuilt the first locomotive into a 4-8-0. Three years later, it modified the second one as the railroad industry's first 2-8-2. The rear driving wheels had no flanges, and the trailing truck did not swivel. It appears that the second pair of drivers was removed and the rearmost three axles moved forward to accommodate the trailing truck in an extension of the engine's frames.

Baldwin built the first "new" 2-8-2s for Mexico's Interoceánico Railroad in 1890, ten of them with outside frames. They burned wood, which required a large firebox placed behind the rear driving wheels, and a trailing truck was added to support the overhanging weight. Evidently, the railroad didn't like the rear trucks for some unknown reason, and it removed them soon after the engines went into service.

Baldwin Locomotive Works

7

Louis Southwestern and Kansas City Southern. In the west, the Northwestern Pacific and Spokane, Portland & Seattle did not go the way of the 2-8-2. Although some instances are inexplicable, these were in general railroads which utilized 2-8-0s, and later acquired locomotives much larger than a 2-8-2.

VALVE GEARS

The overwhelming majority of 2-8-2s had either Walschaerts or Baker valve gear. Other types were applied, and the following general discussion briefly describes each type. In this discussion, the descriptions apply to one side only of the locomotive.

Stephenson

Two eccentrics were mounted on the main axle, one for forward motion, the other for reverse. A rod from each eccentric was connected to a slotted link encasing a block attached to a lever which moved the valve. When the engineer raised or lowered the link, the valve cutoff was changed from full forward to full reverse. All of the mechanism was located between the engine's frames, an inaccessible and very dirty place. It was the first valve gear and it was applied only to the earliest and lightest 2-8-2s.

Walschaerts

A single eccentric crank, mounted on the main driver crankpin, was connected to the bottom of an oscillating link housing a block which was connected to the valve stem. In the most common arrangement, the block was at the bottom of the link for forward motion, and as the engineer raised the block, the cutoff was decreased. This was a sturdy mechanism, and it was applied to a great many 2-8-2s over their life spans.

Young

Resembling the Walschaerts gear, the link was moved by a rod attached to the crosshead wrist pin. Only a few 2-8-2s were equipped with this valve gear which was too complicated mechanically in addition to its operational difficulties.

Baker

This rugged mechanism, comprised entirely of levers and pins, eliminated the exposed sliding parts of other valve gears. It was operated by an eccentric crank mounted on the main crank pin. Cutoff and direction were changed when the engineer altered the position of the principal supporting lever. Though introduced after other valve gears, it became very popular because of its low maintenance and long valve movement. It was used on all USRA locomotives, excepting the 2-10-2s.

Southern

In this valve gear, a stationary slotted link was mounted horizontally with the link block's position controlled by the engineer. Two vertical rods were connected to one end of an eccentric-rod rod whose other end was attached to an eccentric crank on the main pin. Movement of the link block altered the cutoff and direction of operation. Although this valve gear's motion was affected by vertical movement of the main axle, it was extensively applied to Southern Railway locomotives, as well as to both models of USRA 2-10-2s. Only a few 2-8-2s were equipped with this valve gear.

Caprotti

Gear-driven from the main axle, this shifting cam mechanism was mounted between the frames behind the cylinders. Valves were of the poppet type. Although it gave excellent valve events, the whole arrangement was too light for American railroads. Only one 2-8-2 was equipped with it.

USRA LOCOMOTIVES

The United States Railroad Administration produced twelve standard locomotive designs embracing eight wheel arrangements. Over a 16-month period, 1856 locomotives were built, the first one having been a light 2-8-2 in July 1918. The last of 625 light and 233 heavy 2-8-2s were delivered in October 1919.

USRA locomotives were constructed in American, Baldwin, and Lima plants according to orders placed by the USRA in coordination with orders for war materiel placed by other federal departments. They were delivered to those railroads which required additional motive power to handle the traffic of World War I.

Many railroads did not need or want USRA locomotives even though the dimensional differences between "railroad standard" and "USRA standard" were not significant. These 2-8-2s were well received by the railroads, and they performed excellently. Proof of their success was the large quantity of USRA duplicates which were ordered afterward by the railroads themselves.

SUPER POWER

Contrary to common belief, the "Super Power" era actually commenced in 1922 with a 2-8-2, and not with a 2-8-4. The initial locomotive was Michigan Central No. 8000. This significant and fundamental improvement in locomotive design was the doubling of the customary amount of superheating area for each square foot of evaporative area in the firebox and flues. While it is true that other locomotives, like Super Power engines, were equipped with feedwater heaters, front-end throttles, Baker valve gear and trailing truck boosters, it was Lima's designer, Will Woodard, who made this important increase in superheating area.

Hence, when the locomotive was worked with full-open throttle, the steam was much hotter and would release more energy during its expansion in the cylinders. In turn, this increased thermal efficiency while decreasing fuel and water consumption. Although there were other improvements in boiler and machinery design, this thermodynamic factor was the key to success.

Conversion of the Mexican 2-8-2s to 2-8-0s left the railroad world without a 2-8-2 wheel arrangement, a situation which was remedied in 1893 when Brooks delivered four 2-8-2s to the Chicago & Calumet Terminal railroad for transfer service. They were intended to operate equally well in either direction, for which a rear truck was an essential component of the chassis. Angus Sinclair suggested that this wheel arrangement be called "Calumet" type, but the name was not adopted.

American Locomotive Company

In 1893, Baldwin constructed a most curious 2-8-2 saddle-tank engine for one Julio F. Sorzano, who designed this "Modelo Especial," apparently intending to sell it to the narrow gauge Gran Ferrocarril de Trujillo in Peru. It appears to have been delivered to the LaCeiba railroad in Venezuela. Offhand, the engine looked like a 2-6-4T, with the firebox placed between the rear driving wheels and the trailing truck, but on this locomotive a long siderod connected drivers ahead of the firebox with those behind it.

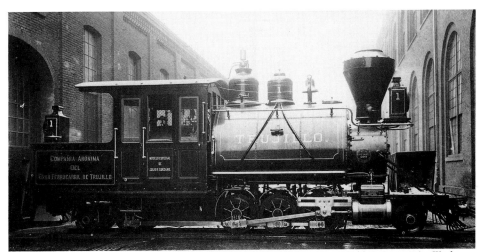

Baldwin Locomotive Works

Baldwin Locomotive Works

In 1897, Baldwin received an order from the Nippon Railways for 20 heavy narrow gauge 2-8-0s, but because the firebox had to be made very large to burn the low-grade fuel, it could not be placed above the driving wheels. Consequently, the firebox was placed behind the drivers on an extension of the engine's frame, and the overhanging weight was supported by an idle axle which did not swivel. Baldwin's sales department named these locomotives "Mikado" type, most likely with the expectation of receiving further orders from Japan.

American Locomotive Company

The first 2-8-2 having a Belpaire firebox was built by Brooks in 1897 for the Central Mexicano. It had very small drivers–only 49 inches–to provide room for the trailing truck, which was soon removed, restoring Mexico to its non 2-8-2 status. It should be noted that the Central Mexicano was controlled by the AT&SF, whose first 2-8-2 was five years in the future.

Baldwin Locomotive Works

Baldwin built the first standard gauge tank-type 2-8-2 for the Alamagordo & Sacramento Mountain railroad in 1898. The trackage of this lumber-hauling line possessed 33 degree curves, 5% gradients and a great double-horseshoe curve. It appears that this engine was the first one to have been equipped with a pivoted trailing truck.

The three-foot track of the Xico & San Rafael railroad ran 69 miles into the forests southeast of Mexico City. Baldwin delivered three 2-8-2s to it in 1898, and two more in 1906, all nearly identical to those of the Interoceánico. Like those earlier locomotives, their trailing trucks had been amputated by about 1910. One wonders if the longer wheelbase was the cause of derailments on the sharply curved and uneven rails of these Mexican railroads. After World War II, Nos. 3 and 8 were sold to the Anahuac Railroad which served industries around Mexico City.

Mexico City. February, 1960.   *H. F. Stewart*

The next 2-8-2 was a 750-mm gauge tank-type built in 1900 for the 65-mile long Jokkis-Forssa lumber railroad in southern Finland.

Baldwin Locomotive Works

American Locomotive Company

In 1901, the Northwestern Railway of India needed so many new locomotives that it ordered eight 2-8-2 tank engines from American, the first 2-8-2s ordered after the consolidated company was formed. Although they had USA-type bar frames, they were equipped with copper fireboxes and brass boiler tubes. The track gauge was 5' 6''.

Baldwin Locomotive Works

The availability of lignite along the mainline of the Bismark, Washburn & Great Falls railroad in southern North Dakota required a large and deep firebox. It was supported by a frame extension and an idle axle. Baldwin applied Vauclain-compound cylinders, the first (1901) of this four-cylinder technology on a 2-8-2. Like so many other compounds, it was re-equipped with two single-expansion cylinders after about ten years of service.

Baldwin built a single Vauclain-compound 2-8-2 for the 42-inch gauge Wellington & Manawatu Railroad in New Zealand in 1901 for helper service. It was much like the Nippon Railways engine, and it was not duplicated.

New Zealand Railway & Locomotive Society

Another new gauge appeared in 1902 when Baldwin delivered a 2-8-2 tank engine to the 49-inch gauge Hecla & Torch Lake Railroad on Michigan's upper peninsula. Two more arrived in 1907.

Baldwin Locomotive Works

American Locomotive Company

Later in 1902, American produced a pair of 2-8-2 tank engines for the Kanawha & Michigan, whose trackage in West Virginia included branches in narrow valleys where bi-directional operation was a necessity. Judging from their chassis, it appears that their design was almost identical with that of the Indian locomotives. Three others, embodying some mechanical changes including the first application of Walschaerts valve gear to a 2-8-2, arrived: one was delivered in 1907 and the other two in 1912.

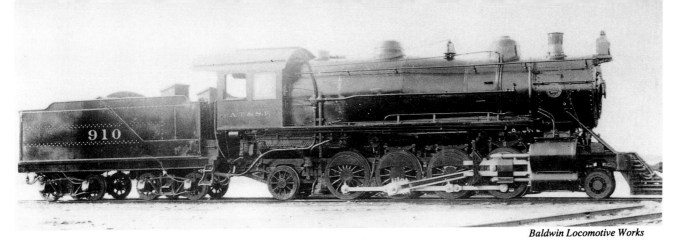

Finally, 12 years after the first 2-8-2 had been constructed, a major railroad–the AT&SF–acquired 15 from Baldwin in 1902. They had Vauclain-compound cylinders and a large Jacobs-Shupert firebox to burn the low-grade coal mined near Gallup, NM. After about six years of service, the engines were rebuilt with single-expansion cylinders, then again with new cylinders and Baker valve gear.

Needing more powerful narrow gauge locomotives than its 1887 model 2-8-0s, the Denver & Rio Grande bought fifteen 2-8-2s with Vauclain-compound cylinders from Baldwin in 1903. These engines had outside frames and a large firebox supported by an idle axle. The railroad rebuilt them to single expansion with slide-valve cylinders around 1908; then again in 1924, six of them were rebuilt with Walschaerts valve gear and piston-valve cylinders.

The smallest commercial 2-8-2 was a 20-ton midget which Baldwin constructed in 1903 for the Hacienda Hornos near Torreón in northern Mexico. It had outside frames, burned wood for fuel, and ran on 2'-gauge track. It was most likely destroyed during the 1910-1920 revolutionary period.

Lehighton, Pa. August, 1925   H. K. Vollrath collection

The Lehigh Valley became the first eastern railroad to purchase 2-8-2s for mainline freight service when Baldwin delivered 27 engines in 1903. Because they consumed anthracite, which burned slowly, their fireboxes were very wide; hence, the cab had to be located astride the boiler. Baldwin produced ten more in 1906, and American Locomotive added another ten in 1907. They were the only center-cab 2-8-2s ever built.

Baldwin Locomotive Works

Baldwin's next order for a 2-8-2 came from the Woodward Iron Company in 1904. It appears to have been designed for hauling iron ore over trackage that lacked turntables.

The apparently successful operation of the tiny Hornos 2-8-2 resulted in the production of two more, identical except for their 2-½'-gauge, which Baldwin delivered to the Conchos railway in 1904. This railroad connected silver mines southeast of Chihuahua with the Mexican Central's mainline. A third engine arrived two years later. Until 1921, when the first 2-8-2s for the National Railway of Mexico arrived, these were the only locomotives of that type operated in Mexico.

Staples, MN. October, 1954.   *H. K. Vollrath collection*

Although the Northern Pacific made quite a fuss about its first 2-8-2s erected by American in 1904, they were no more than an elongated version of contemporary 2-6-2s. However, in having 63-inch drivers, they did become the first 2-8-2s to have large diameter driving wheels.

During the next three years, the Northern Pacific assembled the largest fleet of 2-8-2s, all from American. This brought its total to 180, slightly more than half of all 2-8-2s built between 1890 and May of 1909 when the Virginian's first road service 2-8-2s arrived. The last six engines had tandem compound cylinders, but they were converted eventually to single-expansion resembling the first 19 locomotives.

The Virginian Railway commenced its existence as two separated construction company railroads–the Deepwater in West Virginia and the Tidewater in Virginia. The former company bought two light 2-8-2s from Baldwin in 1905, which became Virginian 400 and 401. The Tidewater obtained three identical engines in 1907, and those became Virginian 402-404.

The Lake Champlain & Moriah's two 2-8-2s, built by Baldwin in 1906 and 1907, were operated without turning on this iron-ore hauling short line in northeastern New York. Actually, they were 2-8-0s with a trailing truck for reliable reverse running.

Like other mining railroads, the Nevada Northern needed a bi-directional locomotive for hauling miners' trains between Ely, Nevada and the copper ore pits. American built one in 1906.

Baldwin Locomotive Works

The Cerro de Pasco mining company's railroad was located in northern Peru at altitudes above 12,000 feet. Its first four 2-8-2s were standard gauge engines with slender boilers and highly polished iron jackets. Baldwin delivered them in 1907.

The two 2-8-2s which the McCloud River Lumber Company bought for its railroad in northern California in 1907 were typical Baldwin engines. They were provided with inside-bearing trailing trucks, Stephenson valve gear, and slide-valve cylinders.

McCloud, CA. May, 1939.   *H. K. Vollrath collection*

The Gilmore & Pittsburgh, an ore-hauling shortline in southwestern Montana, purchased a pair of 2-8-2s like those which Baldwin built for McCloud River Lumber's railroad a year earlier.

Wyno, MT. September, 1940.   *D. S. Richter*

The track of the Kentucky & Tennessee railroad, located in eastern Kentucky, wriggled up steep wooded valleys to reach coal mines and sawmills. In 1908, it received its first 2-8-2 from Baldwin, a locomotive having a large boiler and very small drivers–only 36-inches in diameter.

At this point, 20 years after the Interoceánic engines had been erected, the 2-8-2 had not attained general acceptance by railroad managements. It appeared that they were procuring everything but that wheel arrangement–2-8-0s and 4-8-0s, 2-6-2s and 2-10-2s, even huge Mallet articulateds. The 2-8-2, so it seemed, was merely a 2-8-0 with a larger firebox to burn low-grade fuel, and an idle rear axle which contributed nothing to the engine's tractive effort. It was the brand-new Virginian Railway which recognized that the 2-8-2 was an ideal road-service locomotive. Its staff designed one which was heavier than any predecessor and with a boiler diameter equal to the largest. It had a large deep firebox with adequate grate area for burning excellent bituminous coal. With Walschaerts valve gear and 56'' driving wheels, it was capable of exerting a tractive effort greater than any which preceded it. The first ten engines were built by Baldwin in 1909, and they were so successful that 32 more were delivered by mid-1910.

To recapitulate now, 341 2-8-2s had been constructed by the two commercial builders–206 by American and 134 by Baldwin. Of these, the Northern Pacific owned 180 locomotives and the Lehigh Valley owned 47. Prior to the delivery of the Virginian's engines, all of the 2-8-2s had been designed for bi-directional operation and/or the use of inferior fuel. The design–and the performance–of the Virginian's engines demonstrated that the 2-8-2 wheel arrangement was indeed greatly superior to the 2-8-0 or 2-6-2, and that it was capable of astonishing development during the next four decades. The compilation which follows illustrates that theme for all North American railroads which had acquired at least ten new 2-8-2s, plus some noteworthy examples.

EARLY DEVELOPMENT: 1909 - 1917

Unlike its rival Canadian National, Canadian Pacific preferred the 2-8-2 for hauling its mainline freight trains. One of the later models, the 5185 had been built by Montreal and had an enclosed cab like all the others. This scene was at Guelph Junction west of Toronto in April of 1959. *Dick George*

Bossier City, LA. April, 1934.

All, H. K. Vollrath collection

ALABAMA & VICKSBURG and VICKSBURG, SHREVEPORT & PACIFIC

Baldwin delivered thirteen light 2-8-2s to these railroads between 1915 and 1927. These end-to-end roads became part of the sprawling Illinois Central system, forming the east-west lateral that intersected the system's north-south trunk lines at Jackson and Vicksburg. After some further years of service as 2-8-2s, the locomotives were converted into 0-8-0s because their drivers were considered too small for road service.

Ft. Madison, IA. November, 1937.

ATCHISON, TOPEKA & SANTA FE

The AT&SF was the first major USA railroad to order 2-8-2s. All 305 locomotives of this type were built by Baldwin between 1902 and 1926. The first fifteen engines were delivered as four-cylinder Vauclain compounds, but after a few years of service the railroad rebuilt them to single-expansion two-cylinder locomotives. Shop forces constructed two 2-8-2s using the rear sections of 2-8+8-2 Mallets. No. 1798 was rebuilt from No. 1700 which Baldwin delivered in 1909.

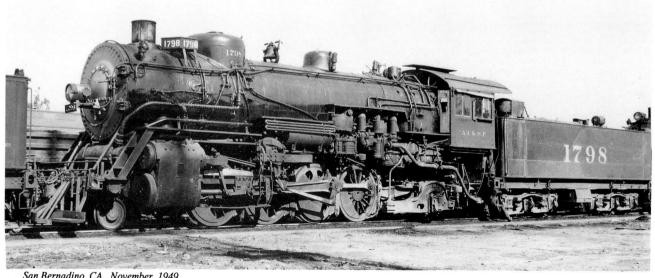

San Bernadino, CA. November, 1949.

20

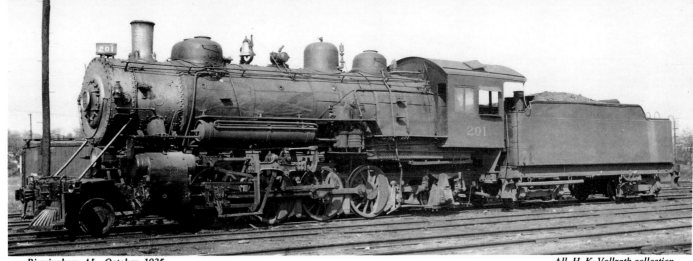

All, H. K. Vollrath collection

ATLANTA, BIRMINGHAM & COAST

Baldwin delivered 17 medium-sized 2-8-2s to this Georgia railroad between 1910 and 1915. They were notable for a very early version of Baker valve gear and a primitive construction of an outside-bearing trailing truck.

ATLANTIC COAST LINE

Because its profile was so level, the ACL used 4-6-2s in fast freight service, and assigned its 37 Baldwin-built 2-8-2s to the slower trains. They were light locomotives of 1911 vintage with small drivers.

Leesburg, FL. June, 1948.

BALTIMORE & OHIO

The B&O possessed 572 2-8-2s, next in number to those of the Pennsylvania Railroad. The first two, Nos. 4160 and 4161, were actually 2-8-0s whose frames and boilers had been lengthened at the Baldwin factory.

Willard, OH. October, 1939.

21

Allson, MA. December, 1940.

BOSTON & ALBANY
All of the B&A's 32 2-8-2s were duplicates of New York Central designs, the first 14 of which arrived from American's plant during 1913-1915. These were augmented by ten more, rebuilt in NYC shops from old 2-8-0s. Eight modern ones, built by American, arrived in 1923. The 1203 was one of the earliest examples, but it possesses a new trailing truck and a switching service tender equipped with passenger-style trucks.

BUFFALO, ROCHESTER & PITTSBURGH
For its size, this coal-hauling railroad operated a large fleet of 2-8-2s—48 of them—constructed by American from 1912 to 1917. Despite their displacement by Mallets, all of these locomotives remained in service until 1954.

American Locomotive Company

CANADIAN GOVERNMENT
Between 1916 and 1919, the Canadian Government's railroad acquired 190 2-8-2s, all of which were erected by the Canadian Locomotive Company, excepting thirty which came from American's plant in Montreal. Commencing in 1920, the CG was operated as an element of the Canadian National system.

CANADIAN NATIONAL
After the Canadian National system was formed in 1920, the CN acquired fifteen more 2-8-2s like those of the CG railroad built by Canadian. And, in 1926 the CN built two more in its own shops.

Minnedosa, MAN. August, 1955.

CANADIAN PACIFIC
Commencing in 1912, the Canadian Pacific built the first 30 of the 194 2-8-2s which were to comprise its roster of that type.

Erwin, TN. July, 1950.   *C. W. Burns*

CAROLINA, CLINCHFIELD & OHIO

Although the Clinchfield utilized three varieties of Mallets to haul its coal trains over a difficult north-south mountainous terrain, it needed 2-8-2s for local freight and mine runs. There was a total of 21 of them on orders to Baldwin in 1912 and American in 1923. The earlier locomotives, with slide-valve cylinders, were veritable mobile antiques.

Augusta, GA. May, 1940.   *H. K. Vollrath collection*

CENTRAL OF GEORGIA

Because it was controlled by the Illinois Central railroad, the C of G's motive power reflected the character of the larger carrier. Baldwin built the first 15 engines during 1912-1914, and 10 more in 1918. The remainder of the 58-member fleet were erected by Lima —12 during 1915-1916 and 20 during 1923-1924.

CHESAPEAKE & OHIO

Because of its enormous coal traffic moving from West Virginia to the Great Lakes and Atlantic ports, the C&O was always acquiring heavy and powerful locomotives. All of its 206 2-8-2s were constructed by American between 1911 and 1926. The first 67 engines (like No. 1111) had 57-inch drivers and a 67 square foot grate area.

Rainelle, WV. September, 1948.   *H. K. Vollrath collection*

24

CHICAGO & ALTON

Built by both Baldwin and American between 1910 and 1921, the C&A's 70 2-8-2s, all much alike, were the railroad's newest motive power. They were utilized on the main lines connecting Chicago, St. Louis, and Kansas City.

Venice, IL. May, 1927.

CHICAGO, BURLINGTON & QUINCY

Like other prairie railroads, the CB&Q possessed a substantial fleet of 2-8-2s, 383 of them. All were produced in Baldwin's works between 1910 and 1923. Except for ten USRA heavy design engines, there was little difference among the various groups, but eventually extended smokeboxes and two kinds of feedwater heaters produced variations.

St. Joseph, MO. October, 1938.

CHICAGO & EASTERN ILLINOIS

No. 1912 was one of 20 2-8-2s which American delivered to the C&EI in 1912. Another 20 arrived in 1918, but they were light USRA models, somewhat smaller than the original engines. Needing more power after World War I, the railroad went back to American for 20 duplicates of the earlier model.

Dalton City, IL. May, 1940.

All, H. K. Vollrath collection

25

Kenyon, MN. October, 1947.

St. Paul, MN. June, 1937.

Proviso, IL. July, 1954.

[TOP:]
CHICAGO GREAT WESTERN
Surprisingly, the CGW owned almost as many 2-10-4s as it did 2-8-2s. There were 37 of the giant Texas types compared to 40 of the 2-8-2s, all delivered by Baldwin between 1912 and 1920. The 2-8-2s were identical except that the last ten were of the USRA light design.

[MIDDLE:]
CHICAGO, MILWAUKEE,
   ST. PAUL & PACIFIC
In just five years, commencing in 1909, the railroad's shops produced sixty 2-8-2s which were near-duplicates of these which American had built for the Northern Pacific.

[BOTTOM:]
CHICAGO & NORTHWESTERN
All of the C&NW's 300 2-8-2s, built by American between 1913 and 1923 were very much alike, differing only in details such as the Young valve-gear applied to No. 2701.

[TOP:]
COLORADO & SOUTHERN
Although the C&S owned five 2-8-2s, built by Baldwin in 1911 to CB&Q plans, they were rarely found on C&S trackage, displaced by a large fleet of 2-8-0s and 2-10-2s.

[MIDDLE:]
DELAWARE, LACKAWANNA & WESTERN
Between 1912 and 1924, the DL&W acquired a fleet of 112 2-8-2s to replace 2-8-0s in mainline freight service. All were built by American. The first 27 engines had inside-bearing trailing trucks and Walschaerts valve gear.

[BOTTOM:]
DENVER & RIO GRANDE WESTERN
All fourteen of the D&RGW's standard-gauge 2-8-2s were delivered by Baldwin in 1912, and were assigned to mainline freight trains until they were displaced by 4-8-2s a decade later when they worked in passenger service. Two of them are seen here doubleheading nine cars of the then-new *Exposition Flyer* through the sharp curves of South Boulder Creek Canyon at 30 mph.

North Kansas City, MO. March, 1947.   *H. K. Vollrath collection*

Scranton, PA. September, 1934.   *H. K. Vollrath collection*

Pinecliff, CO. June, 1939.   *Richard H. Kindig*

27

Arena, CO. January, 1940.   Richard H. Kindig

DENVER & SALT LAKE
Lima built the Denver & Salt Lake's first eight 2-8-2s in 1915. Two more came from American in 1916, the last of which was equipped with a Coffin feedwater heater mounted above the headlight. Ordinarily used on freight trains on the western end of the railroad, they were also used as helpers on the eastern end and regularly pulled the nightly mixed train between Denver and Craig.

Carrizozo, NM. May, 1920.   H. K. Vollrath collection

EL PASO & SOUTHWESTERN
Extending from central New Mexico, through El Paso, and into central Arizona, the EP&SW's main line was operated with a fleet of 25 medium weight 2-8-2s, all of which had been erected by American between 1913 and 1930.

Avoca, PA. July, 1946.   *H. K. Vollrath collection*

ERIE

In a remarkable replacement of 2-8-0s by 2-8-2s, the Erie bought 155 new locomotives during the two year period of 1912 and 1913. The first 20 came from Baldwin, then 45 from American. Lima's first 2-8-2 was in a group of five engines.

Augusta, GA. November, 1934.   *H. K. Vollrath collection*

GEORGIA

The Georgia Railroad, together with the Atlanta & West Point and Western Railroad of Alabama, formed an east-west route across Georgia into mid-Alabama. Their motive power acquisitions, which included 27 2-8-2s, were coordinated in design and timing. Georgia operated eleven such engines. The first ones, constructed by Lima in 1915, were equipped with the rare Southern valve gear.

East Deering, ME. November, 1955.

Allouez, MI. June, 1952.

Jackson, MS. March, 1940.

Richmond, VA. November, 1912.

Bossier City, LA. May, 1949.   *Both, H. K. Vollrath collection*

[OPPOSITE PAGE, TOP:]

GRAND TRUNK SYSTEM
Traffic generated by World War I was the probable cause for the Grand Trunk's total acquisition of 160 2-8-2s between 1913 and 1918. In 1913, the first 25 came from American's plant in Schenectady; 25 more came from Baldwin; and American's Montreal works built the final 50. Canadian delivered ten in 1917 and American added that many more in 1918.

[OPPOSITE PAGE, MIDDLE:]

GREAT NORTHERN
The GN's experience with 2-8-2s was unique in a number of ways. Excepting nine engines of USRA design, all had Belpaire fireboxes, a feature shared with the Pennsylvania and Canadian National railroads. Of the 316 total, 117 were erected in the railroad's shops.

[OPPOSITE PAGE, BOTTOM:]

GULF, MOBILE & NORTHERN
The GM&N's roster was dominated by 26 2-10-0s, but the road did own a dozen 2-8-2s. All were built by Baldwin in 1911 and 1920. The light track of the GM&N ran north-south in eastern Mississippi.

[THIS PAGE, TOP:]

HOCKING VALLEY
Controlled by the Chesapeake & Ohio, the Hocking Valley hauled coal originated on the C&O, as well as that from mines in southern Ohio. Its fleet of eleven 2-8-2s, built by American in 1912-1913, were duplicates of contemporary C&O 2-8-2s, and were exceptionally heavy and powerful locomotives.

[THIS PAGE, ABOVE:]

ILLINOIS CENTRAL
The IC's main line routes were ideally located for the operation of 2-8-2s, and the railroad amassed a fleet of 550 of them, virtually all identical. Between 1911 and 1919, Baldwin and Lima delivered 382 locomotives of this type to the IC.

Easton, PA.

J. R. Krause

LEHIGH & HUDSON RIVER
Connecting northeastern Pennsylvania with southern New York, the L&HR was better known for its six enormous 2-8-0s than for its two quadruplets of 2-8-2s. Though small otherwise, the first four had an immense 100 square feet of grate area. Baldwin built them in 1916, then two years later delivered four more of USRA light pattern.

Delano, PA. July, 1948.

H. K. Vollrath collection

LEHIGH VALLEY
The LV produced the first 2-8-2 by modifying a 2-10-0 in 1884, but did not recognize its road service capabilities until two decades later. Its large fleet of 2-8-2s got underway with the purchase of 47 center-cab 2-8-2s built between 1903 and 1907. Baldwin built 37 of these, the rest having come from American. At one time during the 1920s, half of the LV's locomotives were 2-8-2s. Baldwin constructed the great majority between 1912 and 1923.

Birmingham, AL. September, 1937.

LOUISVILLE & NASHVILLE
A little-known fact is that the shops of the L&N was the fourth-largest railroad facility for building locomotives. Four hundred of them, including 96 2-8-2s, were produced between 1914 and 1921. These were followed by eighteen of USRA light design constructed by Lima in 1919, and 74 duplicates from American in 1920-1923.

MINNEAPOLIS & ST. LOUIS
Like other midwestern railroads, the M&StL had been relying on small locomotives, when it altered course and purchased three groups of 2-8-2s from American in 1915, 1916, and 1921. The 2-8-2 fleet then reached a total of 35, all with Baker valve gear. Eventually, about half were equipped with new trailing trucks and boosters.

Marshalltown, IA. April, 1947.   *Both, H. K. Vollrath collection*

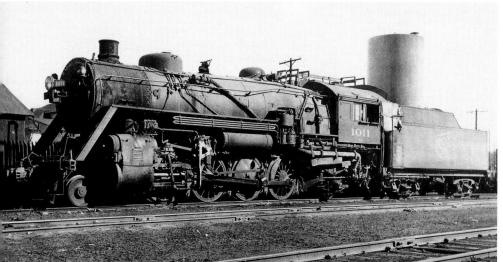

MINNEAPOLIS, ST. PAUL & SAULTE STE. MARIE
The Soo Line's 2-8-2s were acquired in two groups, both from American, in 1913 and 1920. The total of 35 locomotives was divided into ten initially, then 25 later. After World War II, they were modified by the installation of feedwater heaters.

MISSOURI - KANSAS - TEXAS
The enormous traffic increases in M-K-T's territory required the acquisition of 190 2-8-2s within a decade. The first 130 came from American between 1914 and 1918. Lima produced sixty more during 1920 and 1923. The principal difference between the two groups was the substitution of a solid frame trailing truck for the fabricated model.

Waco, TX. October, 1948.

Centralia, IL. November, 1938.

MISSOURI-PACIFIC
The Missouri Pacific system's smallest, though not oldest, 2-8-2s were some tiny engines belonging to its Missouri-Illinois subsidiary. Built by Baldwin in 1917, their longevity was assured by their light axle load, a necessity on the frail trackage associated with the trans-Mississippi car ferry south of St. Louis.

MOBILE & OHIO
The M&O's rails connected St. Louis with the Gulf of Mexico at Mobile, Alabama. This was ideal territory for its 58 2-8-2s, 26 of which came from Baldwin, 17 from Lima, and 15 from American between 1911 and 1928. All but the first 21 engines were close copies of the USRA light design.

Jackson, TN. January, 1940.   *All, H. K. Vollrath collection*

MONTOUR
The coal-hauling Montour owned 25 2-8-2s, one for every two miles of its semi-circular route to the west of Pittsburgh. Only the first 16 engines were new, however, having been constructed by American between 1915 and 1923.

Mifflin Junction, PA. May, 1939.

Waco, TX. October, 1948.

NASHVILLE, CHATTANOOGA & ST. LOUIS
The NC&StL operated 53 2-8-2s, nearly all built by Baldwin. The first 29, built in 1915, were small engines; the later ones, delivered in 1918, resembled the ten USRA light design which came from American.

35

Niles, MI. January, 1956.

NEW YORK CENTRAL
The New York Central System, including the Boston & Albany, Indiana Harbor Belt, and Pittsburgh & Lake Erie (which appear under their own headings), possessed far more 2-8-2s than any other railroad. There were 1337 of them, including 462 rebuilt from 2-8-0s by the NYC's shops as illustrated here by No. 1370.

New Haven, CT. October, 1946.   *Both, H. K. Vollrath collection*

NEW YORK, NEW HAVEN & HARTFORD
In 1916, the NYNH&H ordered its first 2-8-2s. American filled the order for 25, and the railroad immediately placed an additional order for eight more larger ones. But that was to be all, as later freight service locomotives were 4-8-2s and 2-10-2s.

Glendive, MT. July, 1957.

Both, H. K. Vollrath collection

[TOP:]

NORTHERN PACIFIC
After amassing the nation's largest and earliest group of 220 2-8-2s between 1904 and 1910, the NP paused briefly before buying another 160 heavier and larger engines during the 1913-1923 period. American constructed all of these locomotives. During 1918 and 1919, the NP's shops converted the 20 compound-expansion engines to single expansion, and rebuilt six old 2-6-2s into 2-8-2s as shown above.

[BOTTOM:]

PENNSYLVANIA
Although the PRR lagged other major railroads in the usage of the 2-8-2, it very quickly amassed the second largest fleet of them–579 locomotives– between 1914 and 1919. Pennsylvania's shops constructed 344 engines; Baldwin erected 205; Lima built 25; and American produced five of the USRA light design. Except for the last five, all of the 2-8-2s had Belpaire fireboxes, Hoke cast frame trailing trucks, and Walschaerts valve gear. One engine received a water tube firebox, and three were equipped with trailing truck boosters. Otherwise, modifications to this large roster were minimal.

Philadelphia, PA. March, 1946.

Aldene, NJ. November, 1931. *H. K. Vollrath collection*

Brookville, PA. June, 1937. *J. R. Krause*

PHILADELPHIA & READING
The P&R's 57 2-8-2s possessed the largest grate area for this wheel arrangement: 108 square feet, the same as that for the railroad's 2-8+8-2 Mallets. After the P&R's shops erected the first locomotive in 1912, Baldwin supplied 56 more by 1917.

PITTSBURGH & SHAWMUT
Angling through the hilly country northeast of Pittsburgh, the main line of the P&S originated considerable coal tonnage which was delivered to other railroads. The railroad was an early user of 2-8-2s, having acquired twelve of them from Baldwin in 1913.

Los Angeles, CA. March, 1949.

SOUTHERN PACIFIC

For its size, the Southern Pacific's fleet of 2-8-2s was rather small. There were only 135 engines of this type and all were built within the relatively short time span of 1911 to 1921. Baldwin built the first 57, American accounted for 20, Lima contributed two, and the railroad's shops erected the last 12. Differing in driver diameter, they were close duplicates of Union Pacific contemporaries.

Topeka, KA. September, 1954.

Both, H. K. Vollrath collection

UNION PACIFIC

The UP's operating area was ideal territory for the 2-8-2, and the system operated 457 of them. Baldwin constructed the first 50 during 1911 and 1912, and they were regularly assigned to passenger service on steeper segments of the main line. Although the design of the entire fleet was basically the same, the others had larger drivers and cylinders with numerous variations in stacks, front-end extensions, trailing trucks, feedwater heaters and tenders.

Norfolk, VA. February, 1950.

VIRGINIAN

The Virginian's experience with 2-8-2s was most unusual. All 49 of them were built by Baldwin, the first six having been delivered initially to construction subsidiaries in the period from 1905 to 1907. The next 42, the first modern road service 2-8-2s, were much larger locomotives. The first of these went into service only 16 months later as the order was delivered in 1909 and 1910. In 1921, the only other 2-8-2 was acquired as a result of Baldwin's remanufacture of the lone 2-8+8+(0-8-4T) into a 2-8+8-0 and a 2-8-2. The 2-8-2's new boiler was mounted on the frame of the articulated's tender.

Chicago, IL. June, 1940.   *Both, H. K. Vollrath collection*

WABASH

Like so many other midwestern railroads, the Wabash augmented its roster with a huge influx of 2-8-2s. Commencing in 1912, orders for 63 engines were divided between American for 35 and Baldwin for the remaining 28. The railroad went on to add 20 USRA light engines from American, 30 more in 1923, and another 45 in 1925.

THE USRA LOCOMOTIVES: 1918 - 1919

The Rutland, whose main line crossed the Green Mountains in central Vermont, received six USRA-light 2-8-2s in 1918, thus allowing use of the railroad's 2-8-0s to haul wartime freight on the relatively level western end of the system. *–J. R. Krause*

Cincinnati, OH. March, 1949.   H. K. Vollrath collection

BALTIMORE & OHIO

B&O No. 4500 was the first USRA-designed locomotive, a light 2-8-2 and the first of fifty delivered by Baldwin to the B&O during 1918. They were ancestors of 625 constructed by American, Baldwin, and Lima in little more than a year's time.

Mauch Chunk, PA.   Railroad Avenue Enterprises

CENTRAL RAILROAD OF NEW JERSEY

There were eighty-six 2-8-2s in CNJ's fleet of steam locomotives. Following delivery of ten of the USRA heavy design, the road went on to receive ones with larger fireboxes and integral-frame trailing trucks.

Byron, IL. July, 1938.

[TOP:]
CHICAGO GREAT WESTERN

At the end of 1918, the USRA assigned ten light model 2-8-2s to the Chicago Great Western. This example appears to be unmodified except for some jacketing added to the upper area of the smokebox.

[MIDDLE:]
CHICAGO, MILWAUKEE, ST. PAUL & PACIFIC

As the 1920s opened, huge orders of 200 2-8-2s from Baldwin and 100 of the USRA-heavy type from American made the CMStP&P a major operator of the type.

[BOTTOM:]
CHICAGO, ST. PAUL, MINNEAPOLIS & OMAHA

The first group of 2-8-2s, all like No. 402, came from American, with deliveries spread from 1913 through 1916. Ten more, of heavy USRA design, were produced by American in 1919 and 1921. The last eight locomotives, bringing the total to 50, were modern versions of the USRA model. They were equipped with one-piece trailing truck frames, front-end throttle, and pilot-mounted air pump. Note that the 402 has received a complete set of Boxpok driving wheel centers.

Faithorn, IL. June, 1950.

Elroy, WI. June, 1952.

ERIE
Several of the USRA-heavy models which came from American in 1918 received rectangular tenders with six-wheel trucks to replace the smaller, original ones having four-wheel trucks.

Secaucus, NJ. May, 1949.   *Both, H. K. Vollrath collection*

Wichita Falls, TX. September, 1954.

FT. WORTH & DENVER
As Colorado & Southern's Texas subsidiary, the Fort Worth & Denver utilized 45 2-8-2s, all but ten of them older than Nos. 451-455, USRA-heavy design, which Baldwin erected in 1919.

East Deering, ME. October, 1955.

GRAND TRUNK SYSTEM
The last twenty-five percent of this system's fleet of 2-8-2s consisted of the USRA light design constructed by American at its Schenectady works.

Rigby, ME. May, 1942.   *Both, H. K. Vollrath collection*

MAINE CENTRAL
As its name implies, MEC's trackage covered the developed areas of Maine, a territory well suited to 2-8-2s. The MEC acquired 32 of them from American in small groups between 1914 and 1924. Six of them, delivered in 1919, were of USRA light design.

MISSOURI PACIFIC

More numerous than any other wheel arrangement on its roster, the MP's total number of 2-8-2s came to 296. There were only three models plus one engine which had three cylinders. The largest group consisted of 170 engines which American delivered between 1921 and 1925. They were improved USRA heavy design with larger boilers and cast frame trailing trucks. Most of these were equipped with Walschaerts valve gear, and several received trailing truck boosters.

Peoria, IL. June, 1950.

NEW YORK, CHICAGO & ST. LOUIS
The Nickel Plate's fifteen USRA-light model 2-8-2s had been purchased by the Lake Erie & Western, a New York Central subsidiary at the time. When the LE&W was sold to the NYC&StL in 1924, these standard locomotives were included in the package.

Cincinnati, OH. May, 1936.   *Both, H. K. Vollrath collection*

PENNSYLVANIA
A little less than one percent of the PRR's 579 2-8-2s were built to the USRA light design. These five locomotives erected by American were conspicuous in the fleet by the absence of Belpaire fireboxes, Hoke cast frame trailing trucks and Walschaerts valve gear.

Fort Smith, AR. July, 1949.

All, H. K. Vollrath collection

SAINT LOUIS-SAN FRANCISCO
The SLSF did not have any 2-8-2s until 1920, when it acquired 33 light USRA locomotives from other railroads which did not want them. The railroad eventually replaced their Hodges trailing trucks with booster-equipped Delta-type cast-frame trucks.

SEABOARD AIR LINE
Contrasting sharply with its rival, the Altantic Coast Line, the SAL operated a fleet of 161 new 2-8-2s, the first eighteen of which had been built by American in 1914. These were followed by ten more of USRA-light design in 1918. During the post-World War I expansion, 1922-1926, the railroad acquired 134 2-8-2s, all from Baldwin excepting twenty from American, all but a few having been equipped with trailing truck boosters.

Richmond, VA. September, 1946.

Atlanta, GA. May, 1948.

SOUTHERN
The Southern's fleet of 2-8-2s, 326 of them, was exceeded in number by that of competitor Louisville & Nashville's 355. The first group came from Baldwin between 1911 and 1917, excepting six Americans and six Limas. The next 25 arrived in 1918 from American, all USRA-light locomotives. They were followed by 45 duplicates during 1922 and 1923, again from American.

TEXAS & PACIFIC

Dwarfed in size and number by its 70-engine fleet of 2-10-4s, the T&P's eleven 2-8-2s, all from Baldwin in 1919, were the railroad's only USRA locomotives.

Shreveport, LA. June, 1949.   *H. K. Vollrath collection*

UNION PACIFIC

Union Pacific's newest 2-8-2s were a group of twenty USRA-light engines delivered by American in 1918. All of them received Boxpok main driver centers and very large stacks to improve combustion. At the end of the steam era, they worked out of Denver on branch line runs.

Sandown, CO. April, 1952.   *Richard H. Kindig*

Rook, PA. July, 1940.   *H. K. Vollrath collection*

WHEELING & LAKE ERIE

In 1918, American delivered the first 20 USRA heavy 2-8-2s to W&LE. Though differing greatly in appearance, they were close dimensional relatives of the Pennsylvania's design of 1914.

THE ULTIMATE 2-8-2: 1920 - 1949

Led by No. 4610, a pair of B&O's latest 2-8-2s scooted through southeastern Pennsylvania with a long merchandise train. These engines hauled mainline freight for thirty years and were superseded by diesel-electric units rather than by larger steam locomotives.

—Railroad Avenue Enterprises collection

AKRON, CANTON & YOUNGSTOWN

Although this east-west railroad across central Ohio owned only seven new 2-8-2s, all built by Lima between 1926 and 1944, the last one, No. 406, was the last 2-8-2 constructed by a domestic builder for a USA railroad. Its tender trucks had roller bearings made in the Timken factory at Canton.

Akron, OH. 1946.   C. W. Burns

ALTON & SOUTHERN

Owned by ALCOA, this railroad's trackage provided switching and transfer service for railroads whose yards were across the Mississippi River from St. Louis. The A&S roster embraced a three-cylinder 0-8-0, an 0-10-0, a 2-6+6-2 and six 2-8-2s, the biggest of which was this monster built by Baldwin in 1936. Its 347,000 pound engine weight made it one of the heaviest of its type.

East St. Louis, IL. November, 1936.   H. K. Vollrath collection

ATCHISON, TOPEKA & SANTA FE

Baldwin erected 101 almost identical 2-8-2s for the AT&SF between 1921 and 1926 for main line freight service. Notice the two unusually large sand domes and the Elesco feedwater heater mounted below the smokebox. All of them burned oil fuel and their tenders had large water capacity.

La Junta, CO. January, 1938.   R. H. Kindig

Atlanta, GA. September, 1947.   *H. K. Vollrath collection*

ATLANTA & WEST POINT
The A&WP had ten 2-8-2 locomotives. No. 430, a twin to Western of Alabama's No. 380, was delivered by Baldwin in 1944, placing it among the last five standard-gauge 2-8-2s to be built for U.S.A. railroads.

Railroad Avenue Enterprises collection

BALTIMORE & OHIO
All 135 of the B&O's modern 2-8-2s were provided with train signal and steam heat lines, making them suitable for passenger service on the railroad's steep grades in the Alleghany mountains. In 1958, a twin to No. 4450, the 4434, was the last steam locomotive operated by the B&O. Five others in this group were delivered with Young valve gear, but they were soon replaced with Walschaerts mechanisms.

Edmonton, ALTA. October, 1956.   *H. K. Vollrath collection*

CANADIAN NATIONAL

One of Canadian National's newest 2-8-2s was built in the railroad's shops in 1930. Five others constructed by Canadian in 1936 were the heaviest 2-8-2s in Canada. Unlike their immediate predecessors, these six did not have the usual Belpaire firebox.

J. R. Krause

CANADIAN PACIFIC

The CP's final 69 2-8-2s carried 275 psi steam pressure, the highest for any locomotive of this wheel arrangement. In 1948, No. 5473 became the last standard gauge 2-8-2 constructed for a North American railroad.

CHESAPEAKE & OHIO
The C&O's last 90 2-8-2s were the heaviest and most powerful in the eastern USA, outranked only by the SL-SF and GN locomotives which were built several years later. For twenty years, they dominated the main lines, excepting the mountainous middle of the system, routinely hauling 160-car coal trains.

Cincinnati, OH. October, 1936.

Both, H. K. Vollrath collection

Kansas City, KS. March, 1948.

CHICAGO, ROCK ISLAND
& PACIFIC
Excepting twenty USRA-light models, all of the CRI&P's 234 2-8-2s were almost identical. Baldwin and American built the first few during 1912-1913, but after 1919 American was the sole supplier until the last ones were delivered in 1927. No. 2710 was equipped with a front-end throttle, Worthington feedwater heater, Baker valve gear, two compound air pumps, and a trailing truck booster.

Paterson, NJ. 1940.

R. A. LeMassena

DELAWARE, LACKAWANNA
& WESTERN
DL&W's final 50 2-8-2s were much larger locomotives than its earlier models. They were equipped with Baker valve gear and cast-frame trailing trucks provided with a booster.

DETROIT, TOLEDO & IRONTON

Weighing 370,000 pounds, the DT&I's 2-8-2s ranked between those of the DL&W/C&O and the Great Northern/Frisco heavyweights. Other than those on the Great Northern, they were the only USA 2-8-2s having completely enclosed cabs. Lima delivered these engines during the war years of 1940-1944 when the DT&I moved enormous tonnages of freight over the north-south mainline in Ohio.

Quincy, OH. June, 1948. S. E. Herring

DULUTH & IRON RANGE

Over a period of 13 years, the D&IR assembled a fleet of twelve 2-8-2s. Baldwin and Lima shared an order for six locomotives in 1913, and went on to produce the others in 1916 and 1923. They were the railroad's mainline motive power, hauling iron ore mined in northeastern Minnesota to docks on Lake Superior.

Biwabik, MN. October, 1955.

Both, H. K. Vollrath

ELGIN, JOLIET & EASTERN

Owned by U. S. Steel, the EJ&E's trackage encircled Chicago, performing transfer and switching service. It acquired a fleet of eighty 2-8-2s, the first 55 of which were built by American between 1913 and 1923. Lima added five more in 1923, and Baldwin produced the last fourteen in 1929 and 1930. These were the railroad's last new steam locomotives, and in 1948, twenty-five of them were sold to the Duluth, Missabe & Iron Range Railroad. This was the largest transfer of 2-8-2 motive power in the USA.

Gary, IN. July, 1932.

55

Minneapolis, MN. June, 1953.   *H. K. Vollrath collection*

GREAT NORTHERN

Between 1922 and 1926, the railroad's shops dismantled 67 ancient 2-6+6-2s and mounted their boilers on new 2-8-2 machinery. Then, between 1929 and 1932, it performed the same transplant operation with 22 old 2-6+8-0s. Three more 2-8-2s were assembled from new Baldwin boilers and new machinery. Finally, between 1944 and 1946, the GN obtained 22 new boilers from American and Baldwin, and with 25 integrally cast cylinders and front frame assemblies, rebuilt those last 25 2-8-2s, and thus created 25 "new" 2-8-2s.

Markham Yard, IL. 1956.   *C. W. Burns*

ILLINOIS CENTRAL

The IC's main line routes were ideally located for the operation of 2-8-2s, and the railroad amassed a fleet of 550 of them, virtually all identical. Between 1911 and 1919, Baldwin and Lima delivered 382 locomotives; American, Lima, and Baldwin added 135 more in 1923 and 1924. To these commercially-built locomotives, the IC added 33 more which its shops reconstructed from 2-8-0s between 1920 and 1924. Although the IC operated a sizable number of 4-8-2s and 2-10-2s in freight service, the older 2-8-2s were rebuilt in various ways, becoming more powerful in the process.

INDIANA HARBOR BELT

A subsidiary of the New York Central, the IHB's trackage connected the railroad yards and steel mills southeast of Chicago. Its fleet of 64 2-8-2s started with 25 from American in 1916 and ended with fifteen from Lima in 1924.

Hammond, IN. September, 1938.   *H. K. Vollrath collection*

56

Denison, TX. December, 1948.

KANSAS, OKLAHOMA & GULF
Although traffic over its north-south main line in eastern Oklahoma was adequately handled by five 2-10-2s, the KO&G needed some additional locomotives in 1944, a pair of 2-8-2s. They were notable for having been the last standard-gauge 2-8-2s which Baldwin built for a U.S.A. railroad.

LEHIGH VALLEY
During 1928-1929, the Lehigh Valley's shops modified twenty unwanted 1919-model 2-10-2s into 2-8-2s of considerably greater utility by duplicating the specifications of its new 2-8-2s built five years earlier, though they retained the 100 square foot grate area.

Allentown, PA.

LOUISIANA & ARKANSAS
The L&A's biggest engines were 2-8-2s, which were quite adequate for its profile stretching diagonally across Louisiana. Baldwin delivered six locomotives between 1923 and 1927, American built one in 1928, and Lima constructed five larger ones in 1936.

Minden, LA. May, 1951.   *All, H. K. Vollrath collection*

57

DeCamsey, KY. October, 1946.   *H. K. Vollrath collection*

LOUISVILLE & NASHVILLE

Other than the Wabash, the Louisville & Nashville and Missouri Pacific were the only purchasers of three-cylinder 2-8-2s, one each from American in 1926 and 1924, respectively. After thirteen years of unsatisfactory performance, the MP converted its engine to a two-cylinder configuration. The L&N, however, used its engine in hump yard service for 28 years without any modifications.

American Locomotive Company

American Locomotive Company

MICHIGAN CENTRAL

The first "super-power" locomotive was built by Lima in 1922 for a New York Central subsidiary, the Michigan Central. This locomotive was the first 2-8-2 to be equipped with a trailing truck booster, a device which had been developed by the NYC's mechanical department and first applied to a 4-4-2.

South Coffeyville, KS. August, 1944.   *R. F. Collins*

MISSOURI-PACIFIC
Although the Missouri-Pacific had obtained fifteen USRA-light 2-8-2s from Lima in 1919, the railroad's subsequent acquisitions resembled the heavy design, and American built all of them between 1921 and 1925. No. 1555, whose demise was shared by a couple of 2-8-0s in 1955, was the last active MP steam locomotive.

Fairmont, WV. July, 1947.   *H. K. Vollrath collection*

MONONGAHELA
This coal hauling railroad in southwestern Pennsylvania received ten USRA-light 2-8-2s from American in 1919, then purchased six modern versions in 1927 from Baldwin. Later, 2-8-2s from the New York Central replaced the fleet of 38 2-8-0s.

Dalton City, IL. April, 1950.

NEW YORK CENTRAL

Because the first "super-power" 2-8-2 was so successful, the NYC system ordered 301 similar locomotives from Lima and American during the next three years. It is interesting to note how close the principal dimensions of these engines were to those of the Pennsylvania's standard 2-8-2. The obvious differences were the Elesco feedwater heater, trailing truck booster, high capacity tender with six-wheel trucks, and a radial-stay firebox.

Duluth, MN. August, 1955.

NORTHERN PACIFIC

Northern Pacific's last 2-8-2s, built by American in 1923, were much larger and more powerful than the earliest ones. Boiler, firebox, and cylinders were larger, and they were equipped with superheaters, compound air pumps, and booster-powered trailing trucks.

PERE MARQUETTE

PM's 2-8-2s came in two groups of ten each: Baldwin in 1913 and American in 1927. The latter were equipped with feedwater heaters, Baker valve gear, and trailing truck boosters. They were ideal power for the nearly level territory of southern Michigan and Ontario.

Grand Rapids, MI. July, 1940.   *All, H. K. Vollrath collection*

60

McKees Rocks, PA. September, 1937.

PITTSBURGH & LAKE ERIE
For hauling iron ore and coal, the P&LE employed a fleet of 91 huge 2-8-2s which had been acquired in three groups. The first 40 arrived in 1916, all of them from American's plant. The next 30 engines were USRA heavy models, twenty built by American and ten from Baldwin in 1919. American delivered the final 21 locomotives, which were among the first of the "Super Power" era, in 1923 and 1924. Equipped with feedwater heaters, trailing truck boosters and 12-wheel tenders, they were heavier than their Pennsylvania Railroad or USRA counterparts.

ST. LOUIS - SAN FRANCISCO
In need of more motive power to handle wartime traffic, the StL-SF's shops rebuilt seven of its newest (1912) 2-8-0s into 2-8-2s such as No. 1350. The specifications were like those of the USRA locomotives already on the road and, like the other 2-8-2s, they were equipped with integral-frame trailing trucks and boosters. When Baldwin erected the twenty new 2-8-2s in 1930, they were the heaviest of their wheel arrangement–a distinction which they would retain until 1944 when the Great Northern rebuilt 25 engines weighing 50,000 lbs. more. No. 4206 is an example.

St. Louis, MO. October, 1945.

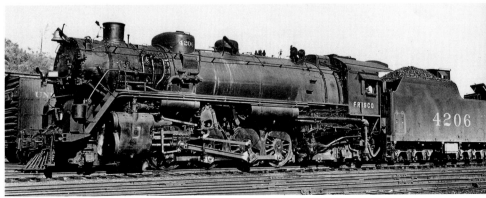

Kansas City, KA. October, 1939.

Alexandria, VA. *J. R. Krause*

SOUTHERN
Between 1929 and 1931, the Southern converted five of its USRA-light 2-10-2s into 2-8-2s without changing the cylinder or driving wheel dimensions, except for one–the 4992 which was given standard 2-8-2 drivers. Although they were remarkable locomotives, the onset of the Great Depression terminated the program.

Decatur, IL. August, 1939. *H. K. Vollrath collection*

WABASH
The Wabash's last five 2-8-2s delivered from American in 1925 had three cylinders, but they were used in freight service only six years when motive power needs declined due to the Depression. After ten years in storage, the railroad utilized their boilers for 4-6-4s erected in the company shops.

Opelika, AL. May, 1950.

WESTERN OF ALABAMA

Five of Western of Alabama's 2-8-2s had been built by Lima in the mid-1920s, all like No. 375. The final one and a twin–Atlanta & West Point's No. 430–were built by Baldwin in 1944. There would be only three other standard gauge 2-8-2s built for USA railroads subsequently.

WESTERN PACIFIC

Because the WP's gradients across the Sierra Nevada mountains in California were no greater than 1%, freight trains were hauled by 2-8-0s for twelve years before 2-8-2s replaced them. The first five came from American in 1918, then five Baldwin-built USRA light models, which were exchanged two years later for USRA heavy engines. Between 1921 and 1929, another 26 were delivered by American. All but five locomotives were given Elesco feedwater heaters, 15 had trailing truck boosters, and six-wheel truck tenders were attached to the final ten.

Stockton, CA. September, 1950.   *Both, H. K. Vollrath collection*

SOME OTHERS

SIERRA RAILROAD
The fame of this California short line revolved around its antiquated passenger equipment and its use by the movie industry. Its 57 miles of rail twisted between Tuolumne and connections with the SP and AT&SF at Oakdale. *Ed Crist collection*

Columbus, MS. January, 1940.   *Railroad Avenue Enterprises collection*

COLUMBUS & GREENVILLE

In a due east-west line across Mississippi, the C&G connected the state's western border at the river with the city of Columbus near its eastern border. Like a few Georgia Railroad 2-8-2s, No. 502 was among the small number of engines to be delivered with Southern valve gear.

American Locomotive Company

NATIONAL OF MEXICO

The NofM's first five 2-8-2s were delivered by Baldwin in 1921, but No. 919, equipped by American with Young valve gear, also came that year.

LARAMIE, NORTH PARK & WESTERN

Primarily a carrier of minerals and lumber, this 111-mile line ran bravely southwest out of Laramie, Wyoming, terminating in Arapaho country east of Steamboat Springs. After being acquired by the Union Pacific, the line's 9055-foot summit at Fox Park, WY became the highest point on the big system.

Willow Mill Hollow, CO.   *C. M. Clegg*

Powers, OR. September, 1926.

COOS BAY LUMBER
Coos Bay Lumber's No. 11 was typical of the tank locomotives which American constructed in the 1920s for the rail operations of timber companies in the Northwest. As these enterprises discontinued or merged with other operators, the locomotives bore the names and numbers of the successors.

St. Johns, NFLD. June, 1943.

NEWFOUNDLAND
On the Canadian island of Newfoundland, narrow-gauge meant 3 feet 6 inches, unlike the usual 3 foot gauge of the U.S.A. The Newfoundland's newest examples of 30 2-8-2s, with inside frames, weighed exactly the same as the D&RGW's 1923 models having outside frames – 156,000 pounds. American supplied the first two engines in 1930; North British added six more during the 1930s. American and its Montreal works produced the remainder until 1949 when the last ones were delivered. No. 1024 was the last new 2-8-2 locomotive built in North America for domestic service.

All, H. K. Vollrath collection

MEXICANO DEL PACIFICO
Because the railroad hauled sugar cane to a sugar factory at Los Mochis in northwestern Mexico, it was only appropriate for the locomotives to burn dried cane residue for fuel. This locomotive was operable in 1988, but it is not known if it is still working.

Chester, NY. September, 1949.   *John R. Krause*

CENTRAL RAILROAD OF NEW JERSEY

CNJ's last group of 2-8-2s were built by Baldwin in 1925. These descendents of the USRA-heavy model had a much larger firebox with a grate area of 95 sqft, second only to that of the Great Northern's monsters constructed several years later. Borrowed by the Lehigh & Hudson River, CNJ's No. 930 storms south over L&HR track with this freight train received from the New Haven at Maybrook.

North Bay, ONT. June, 1953.   *Railroad Avenue Enterprises collection*

ONTARIO NORTHLAND

As a railway of the Ontario Government, this line ran north from CP and CN connections at North Bay. Its main line again connected with the CN at Cochrane, 250 miles north. Mixed trains on one of its branch lines continued the northward trek nearly 200 more miles across the tundra to Moosonee on James Bay. All sixteen of the railroad's 2-8-2s were erected by Canadian Locomotive in Ontario between 1916 and 1925. They were maintained as immaculately as the passenger rolling stock.

Orbisonia, PA. October, 1946.

EAST BROAD TOP

The major user of 3-foot narrow gauge 2-8-2s in the eastern USA obtained all six engines from Baldwin between 1911 and 1920. They were constructed with inside frames, thus differing from those of the D&RGW which had outside frames.

Whitehorse, YT. July, 1955.   *Both, H. K. Vollrath collection*

WHITE PASS & YUKON

Between 1938 and 1947, the WP&Y bought four inside frame 2-8-2s, resembling those of the earlier East Broad Top engines. The last one delivered was the last three-foot gauge 2-8-2 for North American service. During World War II, the WP&Y handled an enormous traffic which required the acquisition off several more 2-8-2s. Seven were obtained from the D&RGW and two from the Sumpter Valley lumber railroad. The U.S. Army Engineers Corps contributed eleven smaller engines which Baldwin had built for military service on the meter-gauge Trans-Iranian railroad.

RARITAN RIVER

This little New Jersey short line handled freight for local industries strung along its 12-mile line between South Amboy and New Brunswick.

MAGMA ARIZONA

Only 28 miles long, the Magma Arizona Railroad hauled concentrated copper ore from mines in southeastern Arizona. Its diminutive 2-8-2 is still in service on a tourist road in eastern Texas.

Oakford, IL. May, 1955.

New Castle, PA. July, 1939.

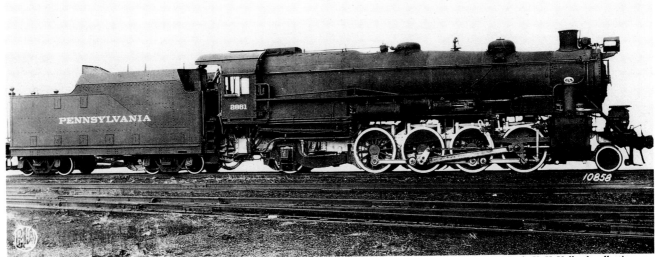

Both, H. K. Vollrath collection

[OPPOSITE PAGE, TOP:]
RUTLAND
Two of Rutland's six USRA-light 2-8-2s are seen climbing the mainline grade over the Green Mountains. They were rarely used elsewhere on the northern and westernmost extensions of the road.

[OPPOSITE PAGE, BOTTOM:]
CHICAGO & ILLINOIS MIDLAND
Because it hauled substantial tonnages of coal that was mined in western Illinois for shipment to Commonwealth Edison's power plants, the C&IM relied on a fleet of thirty-six 2-10-2s. However, for other freight duties it bought three modern 2-8-2s from Lima in 1928 and 1931, the final one being Lima's last locomotive before it shut down for almost three years. In this view, No. 550 was hauling a special which included some Southern Pacific commuter coaches with low-level doors in the consist.

[THIS PAGE:]
BALTIMORE & OHIO
PENNSYLVANIA
The B&O's shops built several boilers with water tube fireboxes, one of which had two drums applied to 2-8-2 No. 4045 in 1927. Five years later, the PRR sent No. 2861 to the B&O's shops for modification with a single-drum firebox. In the next year, the B&O similarly modified No. 4045. When the PRR began to scrap 2-8-2s in 1947, it appears that the 2861 was the first to go. The B&O's locomotive remained in service until 1951. The results of these experiments are not known, although no other 2-8-2s were modified.

Farmington, NM.

DENVER & RIO GRANDE WESTERN

Well known to railfans and the public alike are the survivors of the D&RGW's fleet of 45 narrow gauge 2-8-2s. They were built in four groups, an example of the original delivery being shown on page 13.

After using its fifteen Vauclain compound 2-8-2 locomotives on the 4% grades between Salida and Montrose for five years, the D&RG rebuilt them to ordinary engines with slide valves. After delivery of ten new 2-8-2s in 1923, eleven engines were rebuilt with piston valves and Walschaerts valve gear. Displaced by larger engines in the 1930s, they worked their remaining years on branches out of Durango and Montrose as well as on the Rio Grande Southern. Two of them still exist today, one in regular service on a tourist line.

Hermosa, CO.   *Both, Robert A. LeMassena*

In 1923, the D&RGW obtained ten 2-8-2s from American to replace 4-6-0s and 2-8-0s on passenger trains. Seven of them were requisitioned by the federal government in 1942 for service on the White Pass & Yukon Railroad. The remaining three are still running today on the Durango & Silverton Narrow Gauge Railroad.

Needing more powerful locomotives to replace its earliest 2-8-2s which had aged in mainline service, the D&RGW acquired ten much bigger ones from Baldwin in 1925. Assigned road numbers 480 to 489, they worked out of Salida and Alamosa, and later out of Chama. Nine of them still exist, working on the Durango & Silverton Narrow Gauge and Cumbres & Toltec Scenic railroads.

Coxo.   *Robert A. LeMassena*

J. R. Krause

During 1928 and 1930, the D&RGW's shops dismantled ten old standard gauge 2-8-0s and mounted their boilers on new machinery supplied by Baldwin, thus creating ten more 2-8-2s. Numbered 490 to 499, they displaced a great many ancient 2-8-0s, most of which had been built in the early 1880s. Eight still exist on C&TS and D&SNG.

PENNSYLVANIA
In 1915, the PRR's roster of 2-8-2s was begun with No. 1752, the first member of class L-1. Built at the railroad's Juniata Works, the road's first 2-8-2s had piston-rod extensions, double-guide cross-heads, manual reverse, rectangular headlights, barred pilots, and a tiny tender equipped with a water scoop. Over the years, these features would all change.

FLORIDA EAST COAST
Although the FEC owned a fleet of ninety 4-8-2s, it operated only fifteen 2-8-2s, all built by American in 1925.

New Smyrna Beach, FL. July, 1939.   *Both, H. K. Vollrath collection*

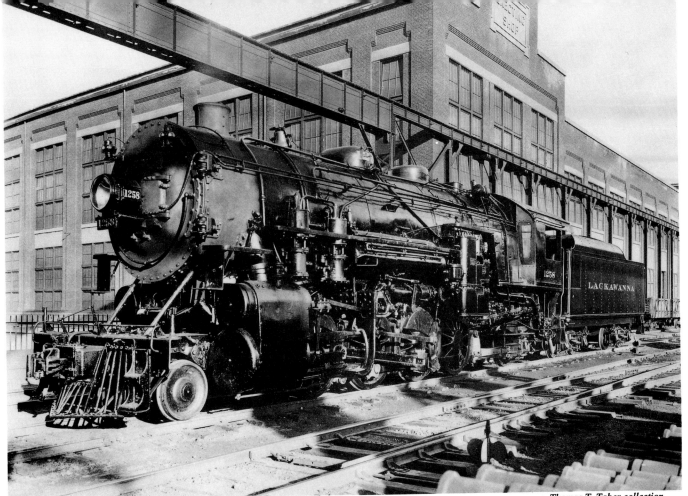

DELAWARE, LACKAWANNA & WESTERN

The DL&W's second group of 2-8-2s were provided with Cole-type, outside bearing trailing trucks which permitted placement of the ashpans underneath the grates. A Worthington feedwater heater was applied to No. 1258 and an Elesco model to No. 1261 but the railroad did not install heaters on the fifty bigger 2-8-2s delivered in the 1920s.

CENTRAL RAILROAD OF NEW JERSEY

Just before Lima ceased operations in 1931 it built several 21,000-gallon, 23-ton tenders which were attached to 2-8-2s to eliminate stops for water and coal on the CNJ's main line between Allentown, PA and Jersey City, NJ.

Bethlehem, PA. August, 1948.

Appalachia, VA. August, 1947.   *August A. Thieme, Jr.*

LOUISVILLE & NASHVILLE
One of the Louisville & Nashville's 96 home-built 2-8-2s is seen performing its customary work–hauling coal from the mines in western Virginia and eastern Kentucky. The service territory where this scene was taken is a region in which the Clinchfield, Norfolk & Western, and the Southern all competed with the L&N.

Iraduato, GTO. March, 1962.   *H. F. Stewart*

NATIONAL OF MEXICO
The NofM's first 2-8-2s, delivered by Baldwin in 1921, were five rather small locomotives with 48-inch driving wheels and a weight of only 180,000 pounds. These were followed by 40 much larger engines in 1921 and 1924, seven from American and 33 from Baldwin.

Palestine, TX. December, 1953.   *H. K. Vollrath collection*

MISSOURI PACIFIC
Following construction of Missouri Pacific's own huge 2-8-2s, ten more were built by American for the railroad's lines in Texas. They were oil burners equipped with Worthington feedwater heaters and front-end throttles. Some had two compound air pumps mounted on the front deck, on others the compressors were installed underneath the cab, an unusual and dirty location.

Railroad Avenue Enterprises collection

SEABOARD AIR LINE
All of the Seaboard Air Lines modern 2-8-2s were delivered by Baldwin and American between 1923 and 1926. They were easily recognized by their cylindrical tenders and compound air pumps mounted on the front of the smokebox. Eventually, mainline freight traffic became so heavy that double heading was required to maintain the fast schedules of trains laden with northbound perishables.

Peoria, IL. June, 1950.

NEW YORK, CHICAGO & ST. LOUIS

In 1924, Lima delivered Nickel Plate's Nos. 647-671, the railroad's last new 2-8-2s. They were rather ordinary-looking locomotives, but they were modified in different ways during the following twenty years until hardly any two were identical. Among the variations were number plates beside the bell, air pumps on the pilot deck, Baker valve gear, trailing truck boosters, and feedwater heaters. Some tenders had one six-wheel and one four-wheel truck, others had two six-wheel trucks which, when loaded, weighed more than the engine.

Lafayette, IN. September, 1940.   *Both, H. K. Vollrath collection*

CHICAGO, INDIANAPOLIS & LOUISVILLE

The Monon's final additions to its all-American 52-member group of 2-8-2s were ten which were delivered in 1930. Though modern in every respect, they worked on the railroad only sixteen years. Replaced by diesel-electric units, they were sold to other railroads still needing steam power.

CANADIAN NATIONAL
The largest group of Canadian National 2-8-2s comprised 75 locomotives constructed by Montreal (American Locomotive Company) and Canadian Locomotive Company between 1923 and 1929. All of them had enclosed cabs, Elesco feedwater heaters and Belpaire fireboxes. Until they were displaced by light 4-8-4s, they were the system's mainline freight power.

Essex, CT. 1993.   *J. David Conrad*

VALLEY RAILROAD, ex-ABERDEEN & ROCKFISH
Celebrating a thorough restoration extending over a five year period, Valley Railroad prepared its 2-8-2 in Aberdeen & Rockfish livery. Before being brought to the Valley, A&R No. 40 plied the 45 miles between Aberdeen and Fayetteville in central North Carolina.

SOME NOTABLES

Highest steam pressure	*Canadian Pacific: 275 psi.*
Largest grate area	*Philadelphia & Reading: 108 sqft.*
Biggest driving wheels	*Baltimore & Ohio: 70 inches.*
Heaviest axle load	*Great Northern: 81,250 pounds.*
Belpaire firebox	*Canadian National, Great Northern, PRR.*
Water tube firebox	*Baltimore & Ohio, PRR.*
Compound expansion, four cylinder tandem	*Northern Pacific.*
Compound expansion, four cylinder Vauclain . . .	*AT&SF, BW&GF, D&RG.*
Three cylinders	*L&N, Missouri Pacific, Wabash.*
Poppet valves, Caprotti	*AT&SF.*
Center cab	*Lehigh Valley.*
Smallest	*Hacienda Hornos: 40,000 pounds.*
Heaviest	*Great Northern: 426,000 pounds.*

Determination of the last 2-8-2 produced/erected/delivered requires some qualifications regarding terminology, which would probably create more confusion than enlightenment. Accordingly, the following chronology will allow readers to make their own evaluations. The listing covers North America only. American (Montreal), Baldwin, Lima, and Baldwin-Lima-Hamilton produced 2-8-2s for foreign railroads after April of 1949.

October, 1939	*Green Bay & Western No. 406, American (Schenectady)*
October, 1944	*Kansas, Oklahoma & Gulf No. 602, Baldwin.*
October, 1944	*Akron, Canton & Youngstown No. 406, Lima.*
December, 1946 . .	*Great Northern No. 3380, GN shops rebuilt with new boiler.*
May, 1947	*White Pass & Yukon No. 73, Baldwin, narrow gauge.*
October, 1948	*Canadian Pacific No. 5473, American (Montreal).*
April, 1949	*Newfoundland No. 1024, American (Montreal), narrow gauge.*

BALTIMORE & OHIO.   *Railroad Avenue Enterprises collection*